ESL Phonics for All Ages

Book 5
Vowels, Part II

Elizabeth Claire

Illustrations by
Dave Nicholson

To the Teacher

Each unit presents one or more "short vowel" sounds with the most common spellings of these sounds. Illustrations of common examples help develop vocabulary, and spelling, as well as auditory and visual recognition. The short vowels are contrasted. A conversation and a song or chant are included in each unit for memorization and sight reading. Concepts of rhyming are also presented and practiced. A Teacher's Guide with answer pages and two audio CDs for this book are available.

Illustrations: Dave Nicholson
Developmental Editor: Nancy Baxer
Consultant: Marilyn Rosenthal

Copy Editors: Samantha Coles, Devin Miles Murphy
Layout: Robert Metz, Samantha Coles
Cover Photo: Corbis Photos

©2009 Elizabeth Claire

Published by: Eardley Publications

Virginia Beach, VA 23456

Printed in the United States of America

ISBN: 978-0937630-24-2

Contents

Book 5: Vowels, Part II

Let's Begin

1. 👓 look

2. 👂 listen

3. 🕷 say

4. 📖 read

5. ✏ write

6. ✏ draw a circle

7. ◯ circle

8. 🔍 find

9. ♪ sing

10. 🥁 chant

11. ✓ check your work

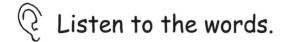 Listen, 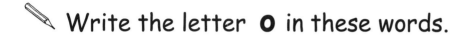 Say, and ✎ Write

 Listen to the words.

Say the words.

✎ Write the letter **o** in these words.

1. b _O_ x

2. f __ x

3. p __ t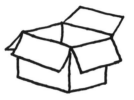

4. d __ t

5. m__ p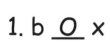

6. h __ p

7. h __ t

8. sp __ ts

   UNIT 1

👂Listen, 😎 Say, and ✏️Write

👂 Listen to the words.

😎 Say the words.

✏️ Write the letter **o** in these words.

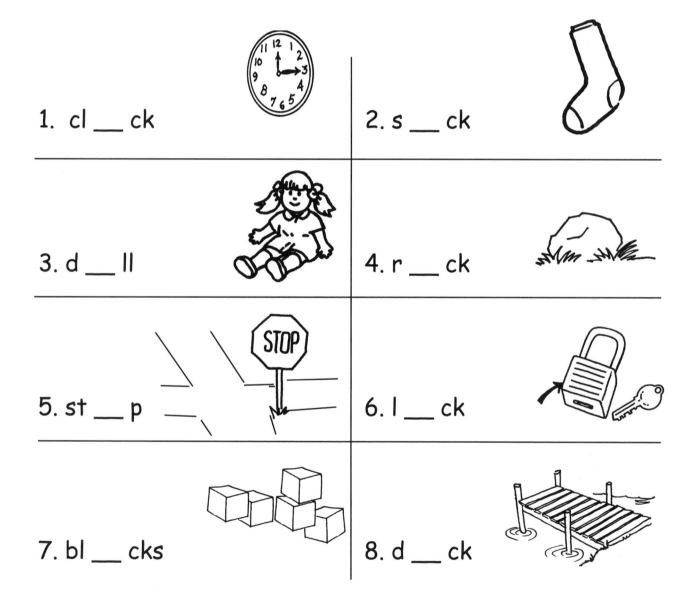

1. cl __ ck

2. s __ ck

3. d __ ll

4. r __ ck

5. st __ p

6. l __ ck

7. bl __ cks

8. d __ ck

👂Listen, 🗣 Say, and ✏ Write

👂 Listen to the words.

🗣 Say the words.

✏ Write the letter **o** in these words.

1. d __ llar 	2. d __ ctor 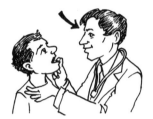
3. c __ llar 	4. p __ cket 
5. t __ p 	6. b __ dy 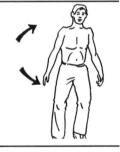
7. __ ctopus 	8. v __ lleyball 

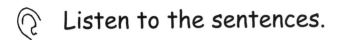 Listen and  Read

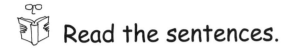 Listen to the sentences.

Write the letter **o** in the words.

Read the sentences.

1. A f __ x is __ n the b __ x.

_____

2. A d __ llar is in his p __ cket.

_____

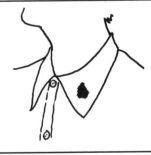

3. A sp __ t is __ n his c __ llar.

_____

4. A v __ lleyball is __ n the d __ ck.

_____

My Bonnie Lies Over the Ocean

My Bonnie lies over the ocean.

My Bonnie lies over the sea.

My Bonnie lies over the ocean.

Oh, bring back my Bonnie to me!

Bring back,
  bring back,

Oh, bring back my
    Bonnie to me,
    to me;

Bring back,
  bring back,
Oh, bring back my Bonnie to me!

👂Listen, ✏️Write, and 📖Read

My B __ nnie Lies Over the Ocean

My B __ nnie lies __ ver the __ cean.

My B __ nnie lies __ ver the sea.

M __ Bonnie lies over _____ ocean.

Oh, bring back _____ Bonnie to me!

Bring _____,
   bring back,

Oh, bring back my
   Bonnie _____ me,
   to me.

Bring back,
_____ back,
Oh, bring back my Bonnie to _____!

👂Listen, 🐞 Say, and ✏️ Write

👂 Listen to the words.

🐞 Say the words.

✏️ Write the letter **e** in these words.

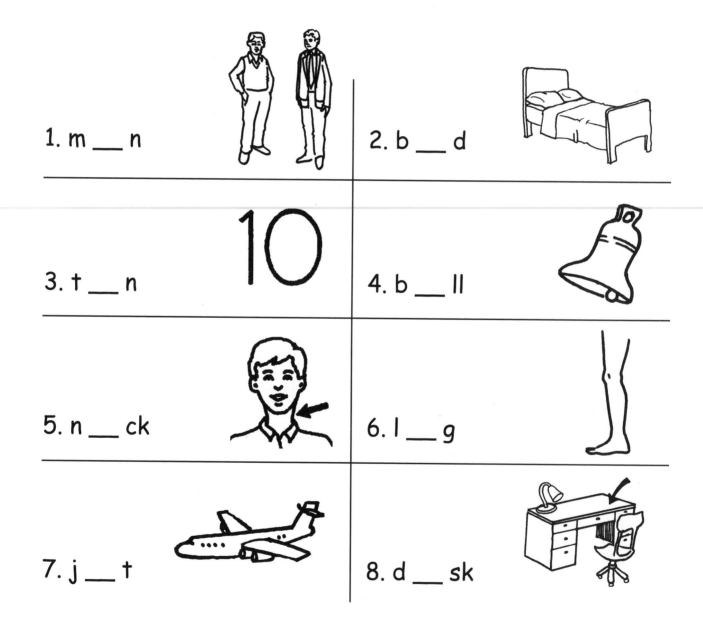

1. m __ n

2. b __ d

3. t __ n

4. b __ ll

5. n __ ck

6. l __ g

7. j __ t

8. d __ sk

© Elizabeth Claire, Inc. 2009 • ESL Phonics for All Ages: Book 5   UNIT 2

⟨Listen, 🐜 Say, and ✏ Write

⟨ Listen to the words.

🐜 Say the words.

✏ Write the letter **e** in these words.

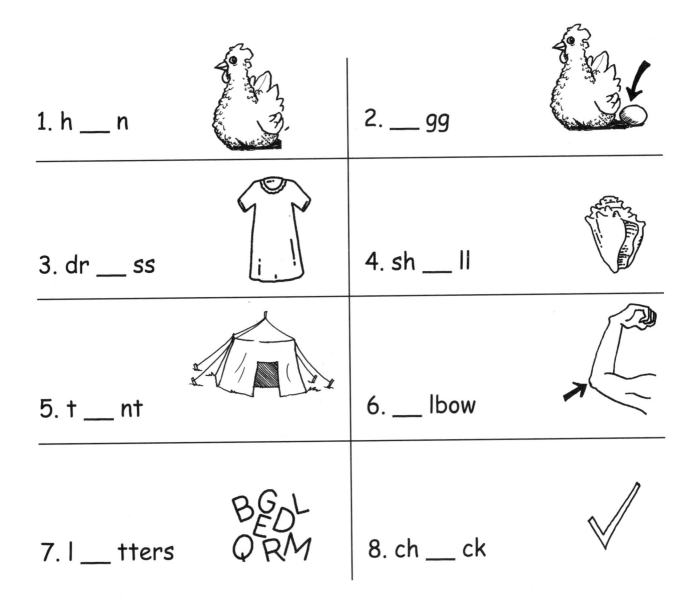

1. h __ n

2. __ gg

3. dr __ ss

4. sh __ ll

5. t __ nt

6. __ lbow

7. l __ tters

8. ch __ ck

👂 Listen, 🐞 Say, and ✏️ Write

👂 Listen to the words. The letter **a** is silent.

🐞 Say the words.

✏️ Write the letters **ea** in these words.

1. h __ __ d

2. br __ __ d

3. f __ __ ther

4. thr __ __ d

5. sw __ __ t

6. sw __ __ ter

7. d __ __ d

8. w __ __ ther

© Elizabeth Claire, Inc. 2009 · ESL Phonics for All Ages: Book 5   UNIT 2

Listen, Say, and Write

Listen to the words.

Say the words.

Write **o** or **e** in these words.

1. __ gg

2. b __ ll

3. p __ t

4. m __ n

5. d __ t

6. b __ x

7. h __ n

8. n __ ck

👂Listen, 🗣 Say, and ✏️Write

👂 Listen to the words.

🗣 Say the words.

✏️ Write **o** or **e** in these words.

1. cl __ ck

2. dr __ ss

3. d __ sk

4. sh __ ll

5. d __ llar

6. l __ tters

7. ch __ ck

8. d __ ctor

   UNIT 2

Rhyming Words

Listen to these rhyming words.

Say the words.

Write another rhyming word.
Use the words in the word box.

				rock
1.	lock	clock	sock	rock
2.	mop	top	shop	____
3.	box	socks	rocks	____
4.	shell	sell	tell	____
5.	bread	thread	bed	____
6.	check	deck	speck	____

Word Box

bell   stop   neck   ✓rock   fox   head

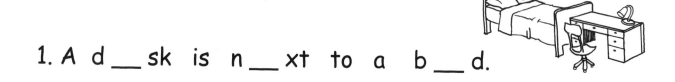 Listen and Read

Listen to the sentences.

Write the letter **e** in the words.

Read the sentences.

1. A d __ sk is n __ xt to a b __ d.

_____

2. An __ gg is n __ xt to a h __ n.

_____

3. A b __ ll is n __ xt to a p __ n.

_____

4. T __ n m __ n are n __ xt to

   a f __ nce.

_____

Head and Shoulders, Knees and Toes

head

Head and shoulders,
Knees and toes, knees and toes.

Head and shoulders,
Knees and toes, knees and toes.

shoulders

Eyes and ears and mouth and nose,

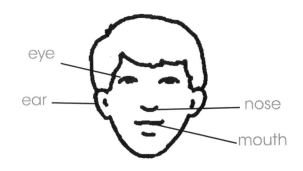
eye
ear
nose
mouth

knees

toes

Head and shoulders,
Knees and toes,
Knees and toes!

☞ Listen, ☞ Say, and ✏ Write

☞ Listen to the words.

☞ Say the words.

✏ Write the letter **i** in these words.

1. p __ g

2. l __ ps

3. r __ bs

4. d __ sh

5. h __ ll

6. m __ lk

7. p __ ll

8. s __ x

© Elizabeth Claire, Inc. 2009 • ESL Phonics for All Ages: Book 5   UNIT 3

✏ Listen, 🗨 Say, and ✎ Write

👂 Listen to the words.

🗨 Say the words.

✎ Write the letter **i** in these words.

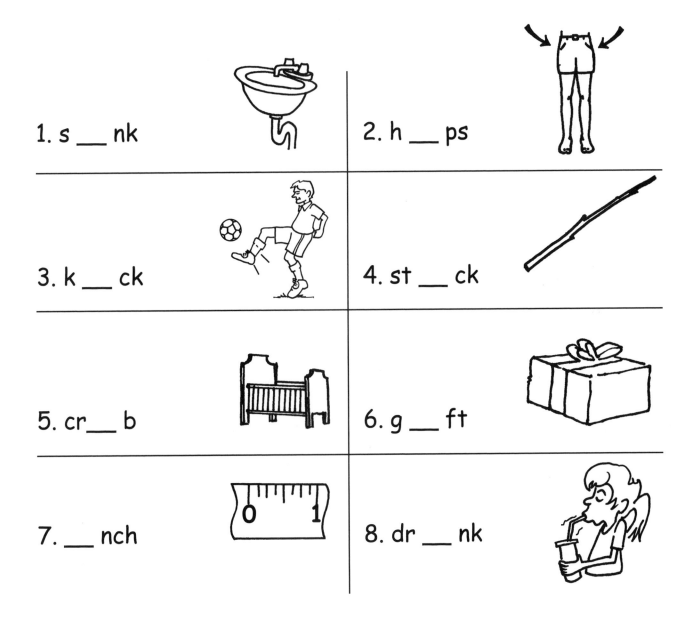

1. s __ nk

2. h __ ps

3. k __ ck

4. st __ ck

5. cr__ b

6. g __ ft

7. __ nch

8. dr __ nk

Listen, 👁 Say, and ✏ Write

👂 Listen to the words.

👁 Say the words.

✏ Write the letter **i** in these words.

1. p __ llow

2. ch __ ldren

3. k __ tten

4. ch __ ckens

5. p __ cture

6. m __ ddle

7. br __ dge

8. qu __ lt

 UNIT 3

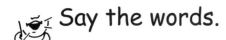 Listen,  Say, and ✏ Write

👂 Listen to the words.

🗣 Say the words.

✏ Write **e** or **i** in these words.

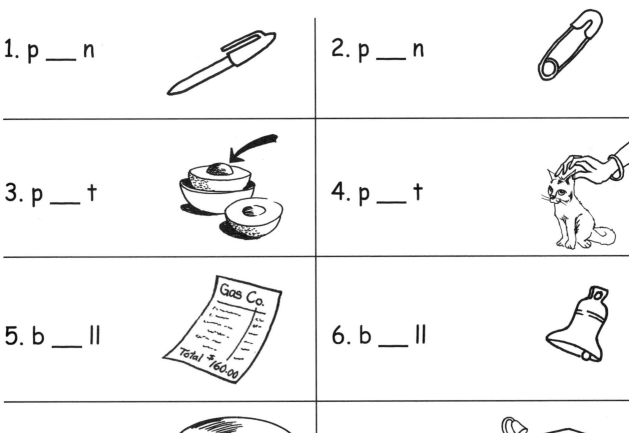

1. p __ n	2. p __ n
3. p __ t	4. p __ t
5. b __ ll	6. b __ ll
7. d __ sk	8. d __ sk

👂 Listen, 🕷 Say, and ✏ Write

👂 Listen to the words.

🕷 Say the words.

✏ Write **o** or **i** in these words.

1. p __ t	2. p __ t
3. sh __ p	4. sh __ p
5. r __ bs	6. r __ bber
7. k __ tten	8. c __ tton

© Elizabeth Claire, Inc. 2009 · ESL Phonics for All Ages: Book 5   UNIT 3

Which Words Rhyme?

Listen to these rhyming words.

Say the words. Which words rhyme?

Draw a circle around the words that rhyme.

1. (dish)   (fish)   ribs   (wish)

2. ship   hip   lip   hop

3. ball   hill   Bill   pill

4. pig   dog   dig   big

5. ink   drink   inch   sink

6. kick   trip   stick   brick

7. pin   pick   chin   win

Billy Boy

Oh, where have you been,

Billy Boy, Billy Boy?

Oh, where have you been,

Charming Billy?

She's = She is

I have been to seek a wife.

She's the joy of my life.

She's a young thing,

and cannot

leave her mother.

Billy Boy

Oh, where have you been,

Billy Boy, _____ Boy?

Oh, _____ have you been,

Charming Billy?

I _____ been

to seek a wife;

She's the joy

of _____ life.

_____ a young thing,

and cannot leave
her mother.

👂Listen, 🗣 Say, and ✏️Write

👂 Listen to the words.

🗣 Say the words.

✏️ Write the letter **a** in these words.

1. ___ pple

2. ___ nimals

3. ___ nt

4. h ___ t

5. m ___ n

6. h ___ nd

7. b ___ g

8. fl ___ g

© *Elizabeth Claire, Inc. 2009 · ESL Phonics for All Ages: Book 5*   UNIT 4

👂Listen, 🗣 Say, and ✏️Write

👂 Listen to the words.

🗣 Say the words.

✏️ Write the letter **a** in these words.

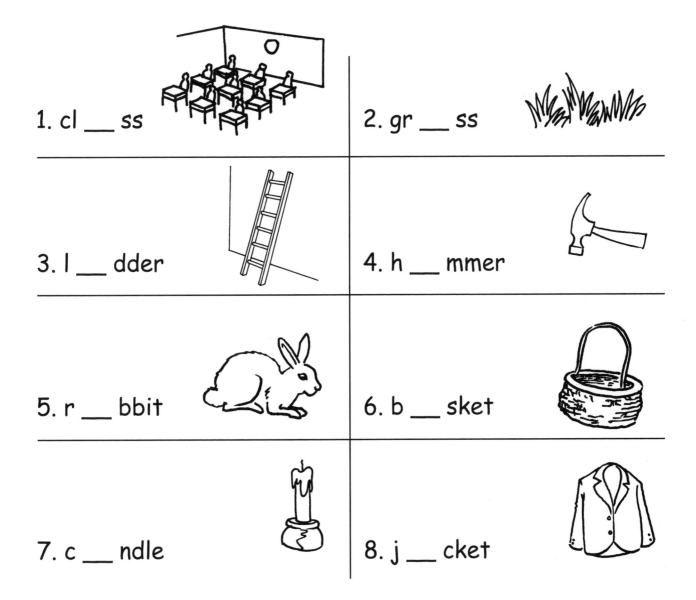

1. cl __ ss

2. gr __ ss

3. l __ dder

4. h __ mmer

5. r __ bbit

6. b __ sket

7. c __ ndle

8. j __ cket

⊜Listen, 😊 Say, and ✎ Write

⊜ Listen to the words.

😊 Say the words.

✎ Write the letter **a** in these words.

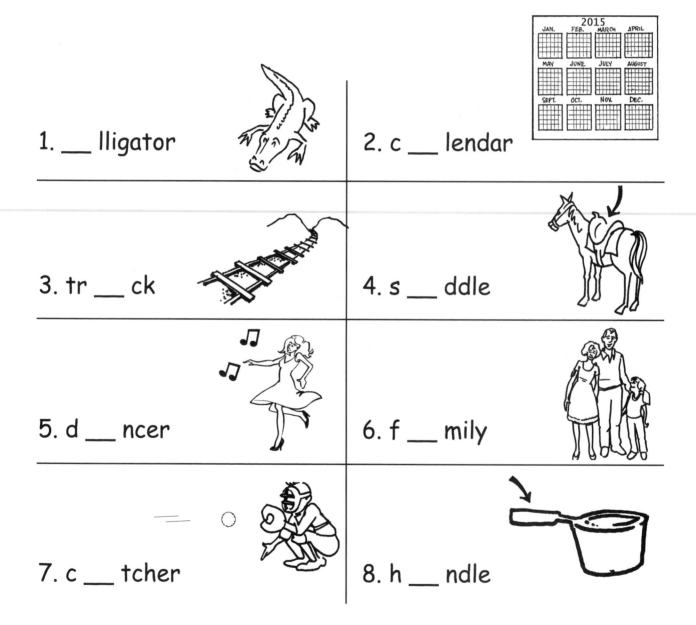

1. __ lligator

2. c __ lendar

3. tr __ ck

4. s __ ddle

5. d __ ncer

6. f __ mily

7. c __ tcher

8. h __ ndle

   UNIT 4

 Listen and  Read

 Look at the pictures.

 Listen to the sentences.

✏ Write the letter **a** in the words.

1. The m __ n   h __ s   a   h __ t.

2. The f __ mily   h __ s   a   r __ bbit.

3. The b __ sket   is   on   the   gr __ ss.

4. The fl __ g   is   in   the   b __ g.

👂Listen, 🗣 Say, and ✏ Write

👂 Listen to the words.

🗣 Say the words.

✏ Write **a** or **i** in these words.

1. h __ mmer

2. p __ llow

3. fl __ g

4. j __ cket

5. k __ tten

6. b __ sket

7. __ pple

8. g __ ft

👂Listen, 🗣 Say, and ✏️Write

👂 Listen to the words.

🗣 Say the words.

✏️ Write **a** or **o** in these words.

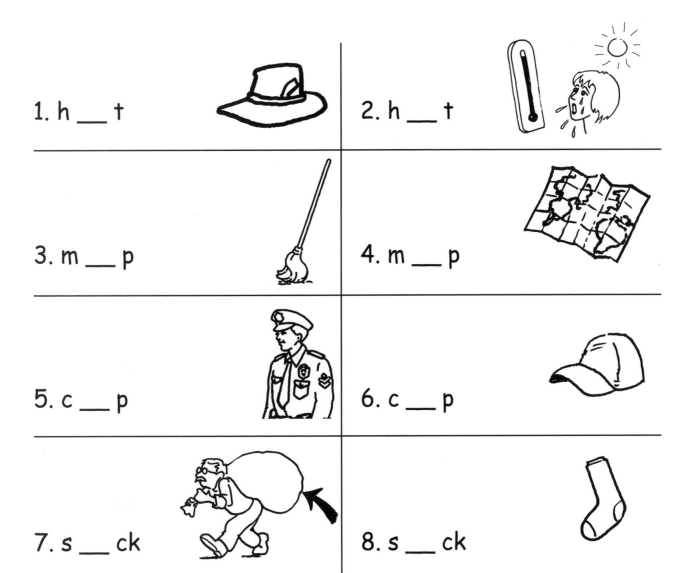

1. h __ t

2. h __ t

3. m __ p

4. m __ p

5. c __ p

6. c __ p

7. s __ ck

8. s __ ck

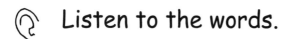 Listen,  Say, and ✎ Write

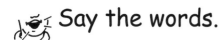 Listen to the words.

Say the words.

✎ Write **a** or **o** in these words.

1. d __ ctor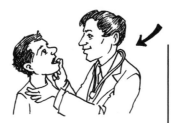

2. b __ g

3. h __ nd

4. d __ t

5. l __ ck

6. __ x

7. c __ lendar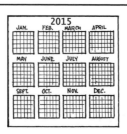

8. d __ llar

© Elizabeth Claire, Inc. 2009 · ESL Phonics for All Ages: Book 5   UNIT 4

Rhyming Words

Say the words. Write a word that rhymes.
Use words from the word box.

1. man   can   __fan_____

2. hot   dot   _____

3. big   dig   _____

4. rock   block _____

5. hen   ten   _____

6. rat   fat   _____

7. net   pet   _____

8. chin   pin   _____

Word Box

jet	✓fan	pot	tin	sock
map	men	am	pig	cat

Writing Sentences

Listen to the sentences.
Write the missing letters.

1. It was h __ t __ n M __ nday.

_____

2. D __ n w __ nt to the h __ n's n __ st.

_____

3. The h __ n h __ d n __ t laid __ n __ gg.

_____

4. D __ n d __ d n __ t h __ ve breakfast.

_____

© Elizabeth Claire, Inc. 2009 · ESL Phonics for All Ages: Book 5   UNIT 4

👂 Listen, 🗣 Say, and ✏ Write

👂 Listen to the words.

🗣 Say the words.

✏ Write **a** or **e** in these words.

1. m __ n	2. m __ n
3. b __ d	4. b __ d
5. b __ g	6. b __ g
7. p __ n	8. p __ n

👂Listen, 🗣 Say, and ✏️Write

👂 Listen to the words.

🗣 Say the words.

✏️ Write **a, e, i,** or **o** in these words.

1. c __ p	2. t __ n	3. b __ d
4. l __ ck	5. r __ d	6. s __ x
7. p __ n	8. p __ g	9. b __ g
10. r __ t	11. m __ m	12. s __ ck
13. j __ t	14. d __ sk	15. n __ ckel
16. m __ lk	17. ban __ na	18. b __ t

As I Was Going to Saint Ives

As I was going to Saint Ives,

  I met a man with seven wives.

Every wife had seven sacks,

  and every sack had seven cats.

Every cat had
seven kits.

Kits, cats,
sacks, and
wives—

How many

were going
to Saint
Ives?

kit = kitten

👂 Listen and ✏ Write

As I Was Going to Saint Ives

_____ I was going to Saint Ives,

I met a _____ with seven wives.

Every wife _____ seven sacks,

and every _____ had seven _____.

Every _____ had
seven kits:

_____, cats,

sacks, and wives,

How many

were going ____

Saint Ives?

answer **One**

© Elizabeth Claire, Inc. 2009 • ESL Phonics for All Ages: Book 5   UNIT 4

👂 Listen, 🐞 Say, and ✏ Write

👂 Listen to the words.

🐞 Say the words.

✏ Write the letter **u** in these words.

1. b __ s

2. t __ b

3. s __ n

4. c __ p

5. b __ g

6. d __ ck

7. r __ g

8. g __ m

👂Listen, 👄 Say, and ✏️Write

👂 Listen to the words.

👄 Say the words.

✏️ Write the letter **u** in these words.

1. m __ d	2. p __ ppy
3. n __ mbers	4. dr __ m
5. th __ mb	6. br __ sh
7. tr __ ck	8. l __ nch

👂Listen, 🗣 Say, and ✏Write

👂 Listen to the words.

🗣 Say the words.

✏ Write the letter **u** in these words.

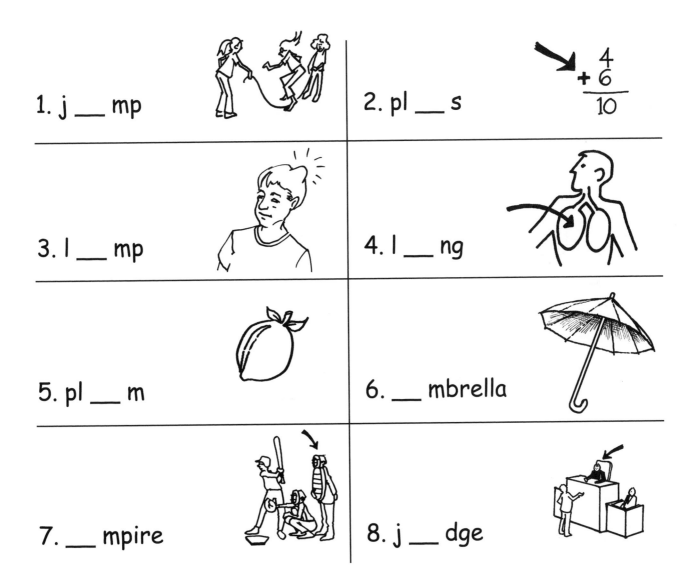

1. j __ mp

2. pl __ s

3. l __ mp

4. l __ ng

5. pl __ m

6. __ mbrella

7. __ mpire

8. j __ dge

Listen, Say, and Write

Listen to the words

Say the words.

Write **U** or **O** in the words.

1. h __ g

2. h __ g

3. d __ ck

4. d __ ck

5. c __ p

6. c __ p

7. sh __ t

  UNIT 5

(ear) Listen, (bug) Say, and (pencil) Write

(ear) Listen to the words.

(bug) Say the words.

(pencil) Write **u** or **a** in these words.

1. c __ t

2. c __ t

3. b __ g

4. b __ g

5. p __ ddle

6. p __ ddle

7. l __ mp

8. l __ mp

👂 Listen, 🗣 Say, and ✏ Write

👂 Listen to the words.

🗣 Say the words.

✏ Write **u**, **i**, or **a** in these words.

1. t __ b	2. p __ n	3. s __ n
4. m __ lk	5. b __ g	6. f __ sh
7. ch __ ldren	8. l __ nch	9. d __ ck
10. r __ t	11. c __ n	12. m __ sk

✏ Write **u**, **e**, or **o** in these words.

13. l __ g	14. r __ d	15. b __ s
16. d __ llar	17. f __ x	18. c __ p
19. m __ p	20. h __ n	21. b __ n ✓

Page 42   © Elizabeth Claire, Inc. 2009 · ESL Phonics for All Ages: Book 5   UNIT 5

👂Listen, 📖Read, and ✏️Write

👂 Listen to the sentences.

✏️ Draw a circle around the correct word.

✏️ Write the word in the sentence.

1. Stop! Don't sit on the _____ !

    lunch   lamp

2. Stop! Don't sit on the _____ !

    cop   cat

3. Stop! Don't sit on the _____ !

    pen   pan

4. OK, you can sit on the _____ .

    bag   box

👂 Listen, 🗣 Say, and ✏ Write

👂 Listen to the words.

🗣 Say the words.

In these words, the letter **o** sounds like /uh/.

✏ Write the letter **o** in these words.

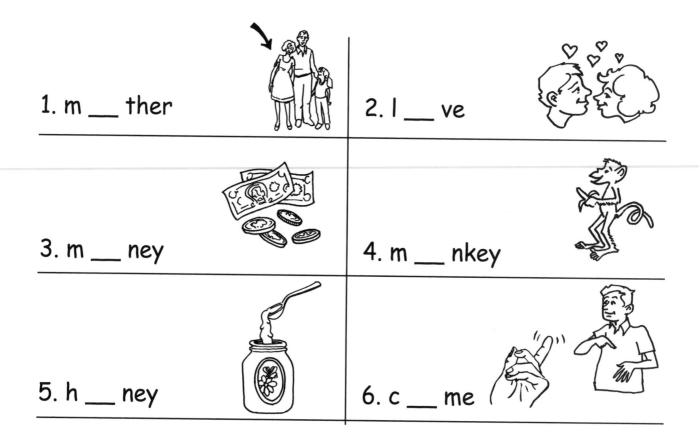

1. m __ ther

2. l __ ve

3. m __ ney

4. m __ nkey

5. h __ ney

6. c __ me

7. I l __ ve my m __ ther.

8. C __ me here, little m __ nkey.

       UNIT 5

Oh Susanna

I come from Alabama with
   my banjo on my knee;
I'm goin' to Louisiana,
   my true love for to see.

It rained all night
   the day I left,

The weather, it was dry;

The sun so hot
   I froze to death,

Susanna don't you cry.

Oh Susanna!
   Oh, don't you cry for me;
I come from Alabama with
   a banjo on my knee.

Oh Susanna

I c __ me fr __ m Alab __ ma with
    my b __ njo __ n my knee;
I'm goin' to Louisiana
    my true l __ ve for to see.

It rained all n __ ght
The day I left,
The w __ __ ther it was dry;

The s __ n so h __ t
I froze to d __ __ th,
Susanna don't you cr __ .

Oh Susanna!
Oh, don't you cry for m __ ;

I c __ me from Alabama with
a b __ njo on my knee.

👂Listen, 👨‍🏫 Say, and ✏️Write

👂 Listen to the words.

👨‍🏫 Say the words.

✏️ Write **u** in these words.

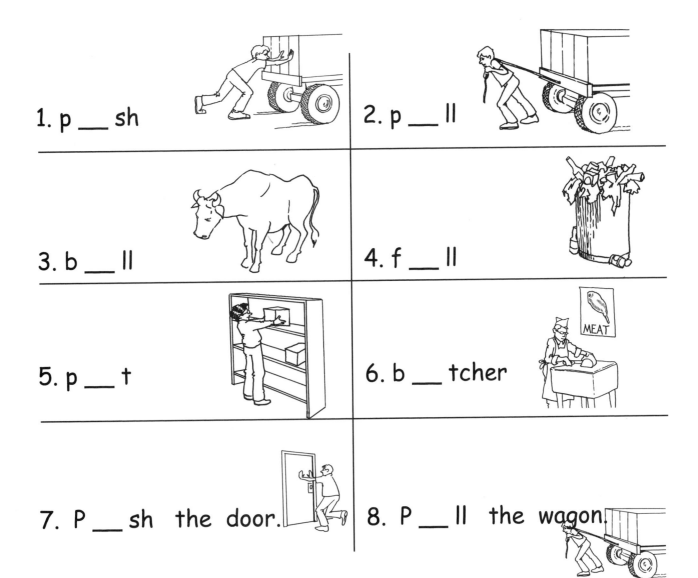

1. p __ sh

2. p __ ll

3. b __ ll

4. f __ ll

5. p __ t

6. b __ tcher

7. P __ sh the door.

8. P __ ll the wagon.

👂 Listen, 🗣 Say, and ✏️ Write

👂 Listen to the words.

🗣 Say the words.

✏️ Write the letters **oo** in these words.

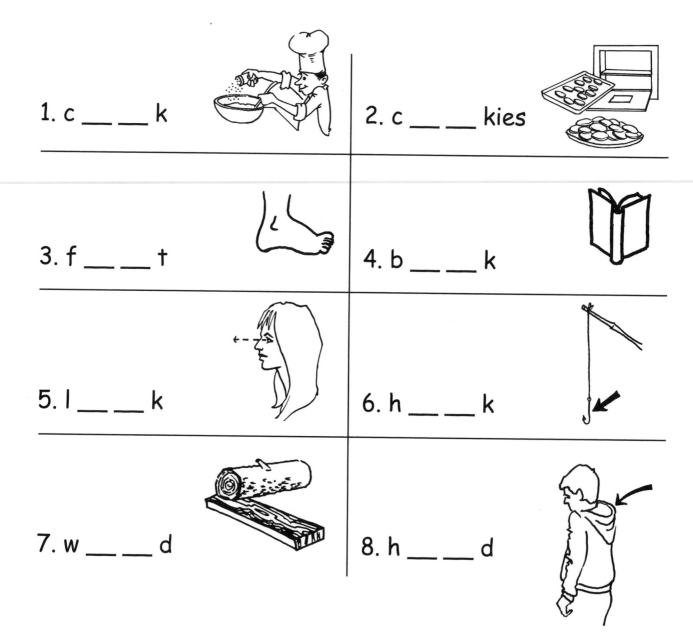

1. c __ __ k

2. c __ __ kies

3. f __ __ t

4. b __ __ k

5. l __ __ k

6. h __ __ k

7. w __ __ d

8. h __ __ d

Listen and Read

 Listen to the sentences.

 Write **U** or **OO** in the words.

1. Please p __ t   the b __ __ ks on the shelf.

   I can't do that. The shelf is f __ ll.

2. Please p __ t   the c __ __ kies

   on the plate.

   I can't do that. The plate is f __ ll.

3. Please put the w __ __ d   in the box.

   I can't do that. The box is f __ ll.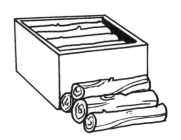

👂Listen, 😎 Say, and ✏️Write

👂 Listen to the words.

😎 Say the words.

✏️ Write the letters **aw** in these words.

1. j __ __

2. p __ __

3. dr __ __

4. y __ __ n

5. see-s __ __

6. f __ __ n

7. str __ __

8. h __ __ k

 UNIT 6

⌇Listen, ✎ Say, and ✎ Write

⌇ Listen to the words.

✎ Say the words.

✎ Write the letters **au** in these words.

1. __ __ gust

2. __ __ tomobile

3. f __ __ cet

4. __ __ tumn

5. astron __ __ t

6. s __ __ sage

7. d __ __ ghter

8. s __ __ cer

Listen, Say, and Write

Listen to the words.

Say the words.

Write **a** in these words.

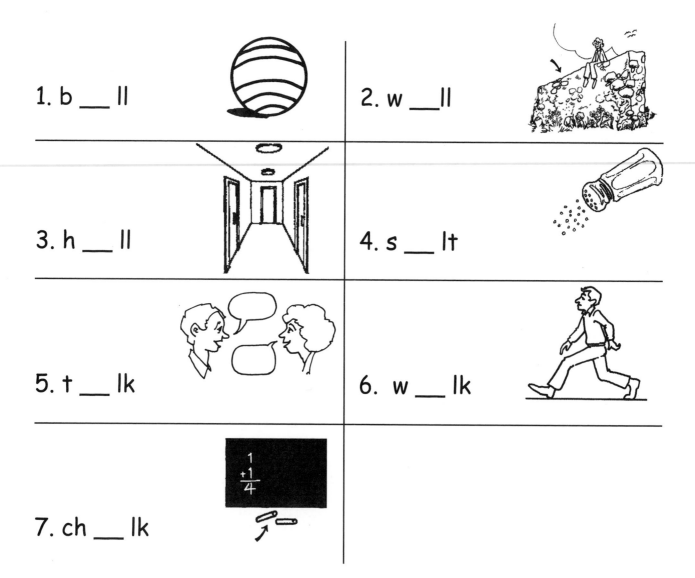

1. b __ ll

2. w __ ll

3. h __ ll

4. s __ lt

5. t __ lk

6. w __ lk

7. ch __ lk

    UNIT 6

👂Listen, 👁️Say, and ✏️ Write

👂 Listen to the words.

👁️Say the words.

✏️ Write **o** in these words.

1. d __ g

2. cl __ th

3. cr __ ss

4. m __ th

5. g __ ne

6. c __ ffee

7. fl __ ss

8. b __ ss

There Was a Crooked Man

There was a crooked man
    who walked a crooked mile.
He found a crooked dollar bill
    upon a crooked stile.

> stile =
> stairs over
> a fence

He bought
    a crooked cat,
Which caught
    a crooked mouse,

And they
    all lived
    together,

In a crooked
    little
    house.

© Elizabeth Claire, Inc. 2009 · ESL Phonics for All Ages: Book 5   UNIT 6

There Was a Crooked Man

There was a crooked m __ n,
Who w __ lked a crooked m __ le.
He found a cr__ __ ked d _ llar b _ ll
Upon __ crooked stile.

He bought
   a crooked c __ t,
Which c __ __ ght
   a crooked m __ __ se,

And they
   __ ll lived
   together,

__ n a
cr __ __ ked
l __ ttle
house.

Listen, Say, and Write

Listen to the words.

Say the words.

Write **a** in these words.

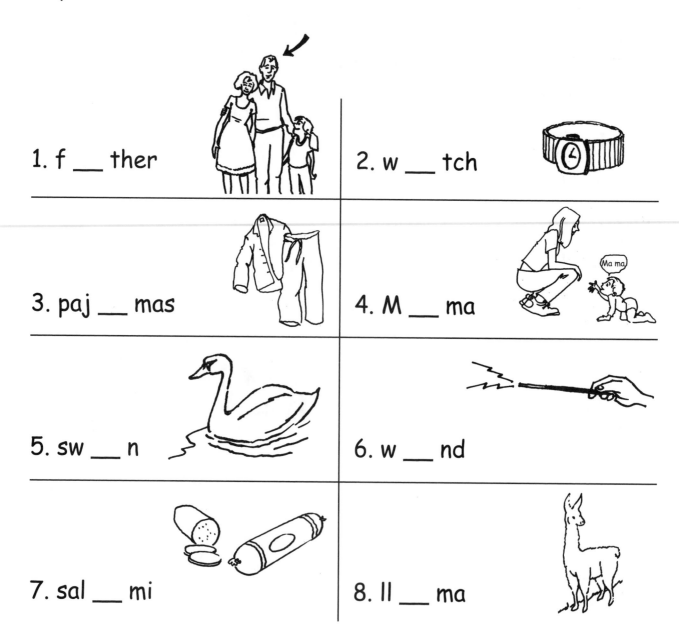

1. f __ ther

2. w __ tch

3. paj __ mas

4. M __ ma

5. sw __ n

6. w __ nd

7. sal __ mi

8. ll __ ma

 Listen, Say, and Write

Listen to the words.

Say the words.

Write the letters **ar** in these words

1. c __ __

2. y __ __ d

3. __ __ m

4. al __ __ m

5. b __ __ n

6. st __ __

7. j __ __

8. sh __ __ k

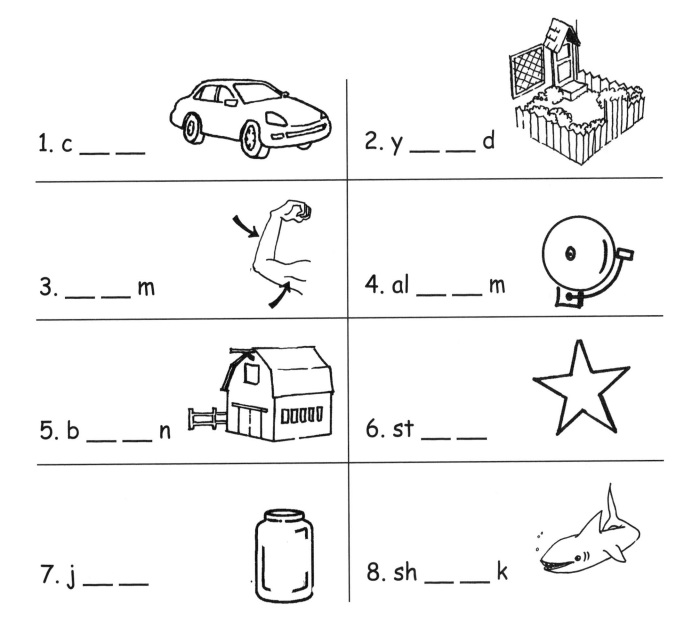

Listen, Say, and Write

👂 Listen to the words.

🗣 Say the words.

✏️ Write the letters **or** in these words.

1. h __ __ se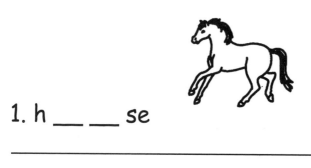

2. st __ __ e

3. __ __ ange

4. f __ __ k

5. p __ __ ch

6. c __ __ n

7. h __ __ n

8. f __ __ ty

 UNIT 7

👂Listen, 😎 Say, and ✏️ Write

👂 Listen to the words.

😎 Say the words.

✏️ Write the letters **ur** in these words.

1. ch __ __ ch	2. p __ __ se
3. n __ __ se	4. t __ __ ban
5. t __ __ tle	6. c __ __ ls
7. f __ __	8. t __ __ key

⌢ Listen, ☹ Say, and ✎ Write

⌢ Listen to the words.

☹ Say the words.

✎ Write **ar**, **or**, or **ur** in these words.

1. st __ __

2. c __ __ n

3. n __ __ se

4. p __ __ se

5. h __ __ se

6. __ __ m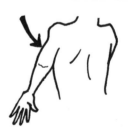

7. c __ __ l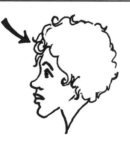

8. f __ __ ty

    UNIT 7

Listen, Say, and Write

Listen to the words.

Say the words.

Write the letters **ir** in these words.

1. g __ __ l	2. b __ __ d
30 3. th __ __ ty	4. d __ __ t
13 5. th __ __ teen	6. c __ __ cle
7. c __ __ cus	8. th __ __ d

👂Listen, 🧑‍🏫 Say, and ✏️ Write

👂 Listen to the words.

🧑‍🏫 Say the words.

✏️ Write the letters **er** in these words.

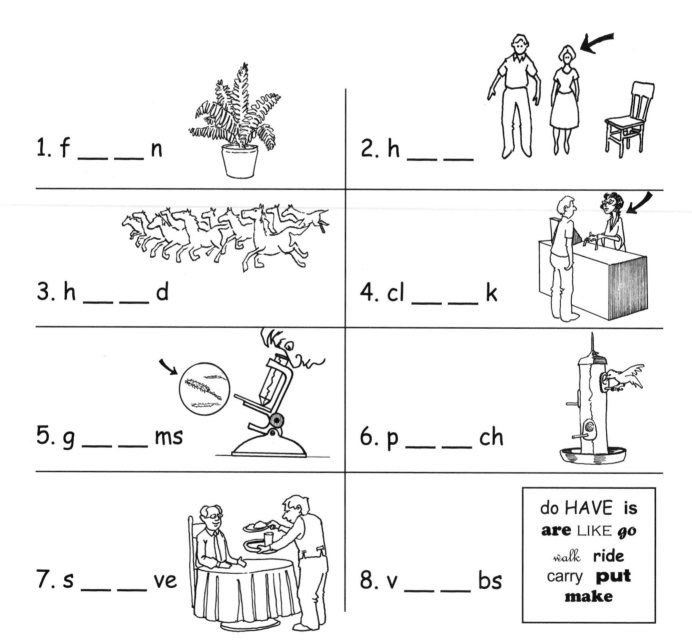

1. f __ __ n

2. h __ __

3. h __ __ d

4. cl __ __ k

5. g __ __ ms

6. p __ __ ch

7. s __ __ ve

8. v __ __ bs

do HAVE is
are LIKE *go*
walk ride
carry **put**
make

 UNIT 7

Star Light, Star Bright

Star light,

Star bright,

First star I see tonight.

I wish I may,

I wish I might,

Have this wish

I wish tonight.

Star Light, Star Bright

_____ light,

Star _____,

_____ star I _____ tonight.

I wish I _____,

I _____ I might,

Have _____ wish

_____ wish tonight.

👂Listen, 🗣 Say, and ✏ Write

👂 Listen to the words.

🗣 Say the words.

✏ Write the letters **ear** in these words.

1. __ __ __

2. h __ __ __ __

3. t __ __ __ s

4. y __ __ __ s

5. b __ __ __ d

6. sp __ __ __ __

✏ Write the letters **eer** in these words.

7. d __ __ __ __

8. b __ __ __ __

⌒Listen, Say, and ✎Write

⌒ Listen to the words.

Say the words.

✎ Write the letters **air** in these words.

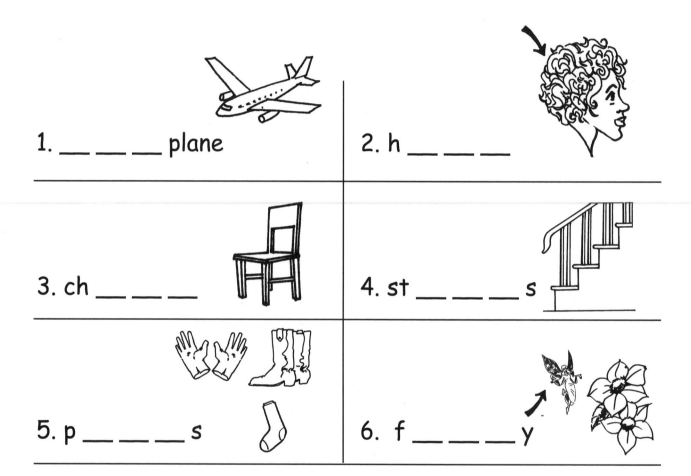

1. __ __ __ plane

2. h __ __ __

3. ch __ __ __

4. st __ __ __ s

5. p __ __ __ s

6. f __ __ __ y

7. The ch __ __ __ is near the st __ __ __ __.

👂 Listen, 😮 Say, and ✏️ Write

👂 Listen to the words.

😮 Say the words.

✏️ Write the letters **ire** in these words.

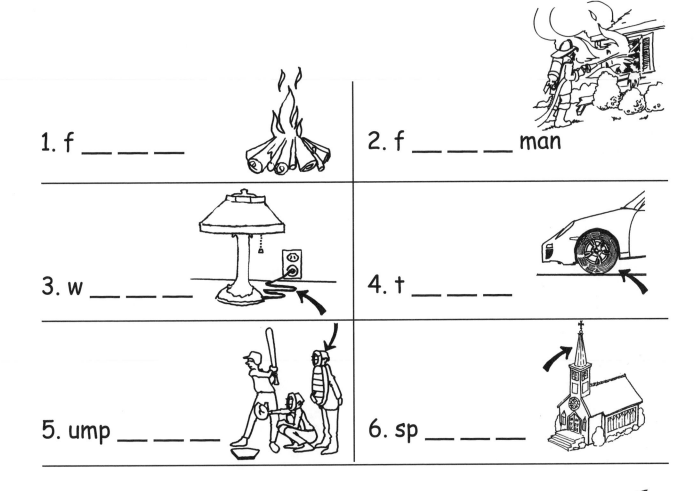

1. f _ _ _ _

2. f _ _ _ _ man

3. w _ _ _ _

4. t _ _ _ _

5. ump _ _ _ _

6. sp _ _ _ _

7. The bad w _ _ _ _ caused a f _ _ _ _ .

Listen, Read, and Sing

Old MacDonald Had a Farm

Old MacDonald had a farm.
Ee-i-ee-i-oh!
And on this farm he had some cows.
Ee-i-ee-i-oh!
With a moo moo here, a moo moo there;
Here a moo, there a moo, everywhere a moo moo ;
Old MacDonald had a farm
Ee-i-ee-i-oh!

Old MacDonald had a farm.
Ee-i-ee-i-oh!
And on this farm he had some ducks.
Ee-i-ee-i-oh!
With a quack quack here, a quack quack there;
Here a quack, there a quack,
Everywhere a quack quack,
Here a moo,
there a moo,
Everywhere
a moo moo;
Old MacDonald
had a farm!

Ee-i-ee-i-oh!

Listen, Write, and ♫ Sing

Old MacDonald Had a Farm

Old M __ cDonald _____ a farm.

Ee-i-ee-i-oh!

And ____ this _____ he had _____ cows.

Ee-i-ee-i-oh!

With a moo moo _____, a moo moo there;

Here a moo, there a moo,

Everywhere a moo _____ ;

_____ MacD __ nald

had ___ farm,

Ee-i-ee-i-oh!

Story: The Turtle and the Hawk-1

1. Once there was an old turtle. He lived in a pond. He looked at mud all day long.

2. The turtle did not like to look at mud. He wanted to see the world. "I wish I had wings," the turtle said to himself.

3. One day, a hawk came to the pond to get a drink.

"Can you help me?" asked the turtle.
"I want to fly high in the sky. I want to see the world."

The Turtle and the Hawk-2

4. "What will you do for me?" asked the hawk.

"I can tell you where to find gold, diamonds, and pearls," said the turtle.

5. "Then I will do it," said the hawk.
"I will take you up into the sky with me."

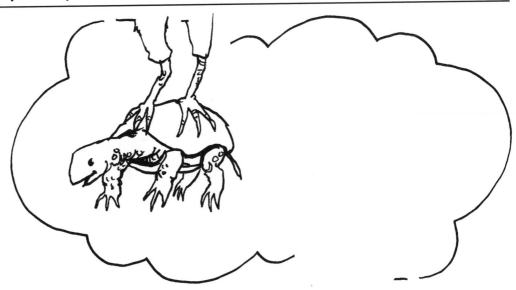

6. "Thank you!" said the turtle. The hawk took the turtle in its big claws. It took the turtle up, up, up into the sky.

The Turtle and the Hawk-3

7. The turtle was very happy to be in the sky.
He saw animals and farms. He saw fields and forests.

8. "Are you happy?" asked the hawk.
"Yes, very happy," said the turtle.

9. "OK," said the hawk.
"Now tell me where I can find gold, diamonds, and pearls."

10. "I'm sorry," said the turtle. "I don't know."

     UNIT 9

The Turtle and the Hawk-4

11. "Oh," said the hawk. "You told me a lie. You are getting very heavy, now, Mister Turtle."

12. The hawk opened his claws. He let go of the turtle.

Mr. = Mister

13. "Goodbye, Mr. Turtle," said the hawk. "Next time, don't tell a lie."

14. The turtle fell down, down, down. He fell back into the mud.

The Turtle and the Hawk-5

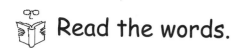 Look at the pictures.

Read the words.

Write the letter next to the word.

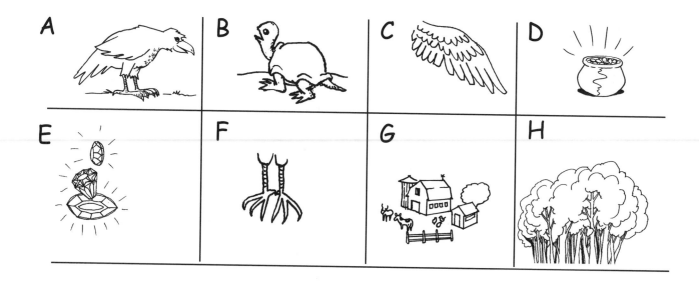

1. turtle __B__   2. hawk _____   3. wing _____

4. forest _____   5. diamonds _____   6. gold _____

7. claws _____   8. farm _____

© Elizabeth Claire, Inc. 2009 • ESL Phonics for All Ages: Book 5   UNIT 9

The Turtle and the Hawk-6

📖 Read the sentences.

✏️ Draw a circle around the best word.

1. Once there was a turtle who lived in a _____.

   (pond)   house

2. The turtle did not like to _____ ____ mud all day.

   fly in   look at

3. He wanted to _____ the world.

   eat   see

4. "I wish I had _____," said the turtle.

   pearls   wings

5. One day, a _____ came to the pond to get a drink.

   hawk   turtle

© Elizabeth Claire, Inc. 2009 • ESL Phonics for All Ages Book 5

The Turtle and the Hawk-7

Read the sentences.

Draw a circle around the best word.

6. "I can tell you where to find _____."

   a drink   pearls, diamonds, and gold

7. The hawk picked the turtle up in its big _____.

   wings   claws

8. The turtle was _____ to see the world.

   sad   happy

9. The hawk opened its claws and dropped the _____.

   diamonds   turtle

10. The turtle fell down to the _____.

    farm   mud

© Elizabeth Claire, Inc. 2009 · ESL Phonics for All Ages: Book 5   UNIT 9

The Turtle and the Hawk-8

Who said it? The turtle or the hawk?

Draw a circle around the one who said it.

1. "I wish I had wings."   (turtle)   hawk

2. "I want to see the world."   turtle   hawk

3. "What will you do for me?"   turtle   hawk

4. "I know where you can find pearls."   turtle   hawk

5. "I will take you up in the sky."   turtle   hawk

6. "I'm sorry, I don't know."   turtle   hawk

7. "You are getting heavy."   turtle   hawk

8. "Next time, don't tell a lie."   turtle   hawk

There's a Hole in the Bottom of the Sea-1

1. There's a hole
   in the bottom
   of the sea.
There's a hole in the bottom of the sea.

There's a hole,
There's a hole,

There's a hole in the bottom of the sea.

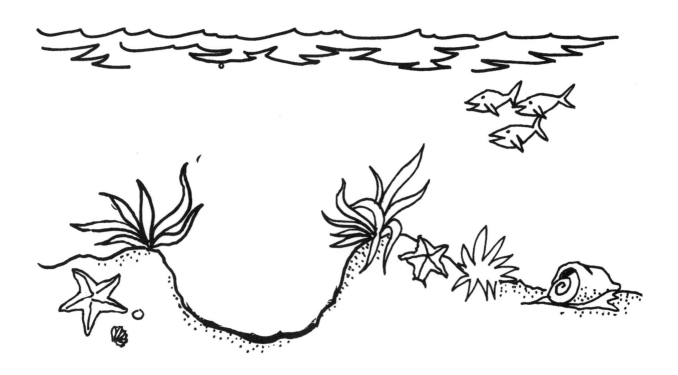

 UNIT 10

There's a Hole in the Bottom of the Sea-2

2. There's a log
   in the hole
   in the bottom of the sea.
There's a log in the hole
   in the bottom of the sea.

There's a hole,
There's a hole,
There's a hole in the bottom of the sea.

3. There's a bump
   on the log
   in the hole
   in the bottom of the sea.

There's a bump on the log in the hole
   in the bottom of the sea.

There's a hole,
There's a hole,
There's a hole in the bottom of the sea.

There's a Hole in the Bottom of the Sea-3

4. There's a frog
   on the bump
   on the log
   in the hole
   in the bottom of the sea.

There's a frog on the bump on the log in the hole in the bottom of the sea.

There's a hole,
There's a hole,
There's a hole in the bottom of the sea.

5. There's a fly
   on the frog
   on the bump
   on the log
   in the hole
   in the bottom of the sea.

There's a fly on the frog on the bump on the log in the hole in the bottom of the sea.
There's a hole,
There's a hole,

There's a hole in the bottom of the sea.

 © Elizabeth Claire, Inc. 2009 · ESL Phonics for All Ages: Book 5   UNIT 10

There's a Hole in the Bottom of the Sea-4

6. There's a flea
   on the fly
   on the frog
   on the bump
   on the log
   in the hole
   in the bottom of the sea.

There's a flea on the fly on the frog on the bump on the log in the hole in the bottom of the sea.

There's a hole, there's a hole,

There's a hole in the bottom of the sea.

There's a Hole in the Bottom of the Sea-5

 Listen to the sentences.

 Write the missing letters.

There's a __ __ ea

on the fl __

on the fr __ g

on the b __ mp

on the l __ g

in the h __ le

in the b __ ttom of the s __ __ .

There's a h __ le, there's a h __ le,

There's a h __ le in the b __ ttom

of the s __ __ .

There's a Hole in the Bottom of the Sea-6

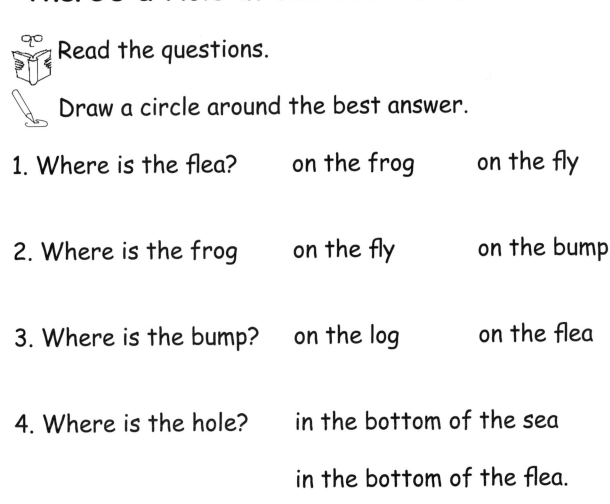 Read the questions.

Draw a circle around the best answer.

1. Where is the flea?   on the frog   on the fly

2. Where is the frog   on the fly   on the bump

3. Where is the bump?   on the log   on the flea

4. Where is the hole?   in the bottom of the sea

    in the bottom of the flea.

5. Write the missing words:

There's a _____ on the _____

on the _____ on the _____

on the _____ in the _____

in the _____ of the _____.

Mastery Test 1

Write the best word for each picture.

cap	cup	✓ cat	coat	cook
corn	cow	kite	key	king

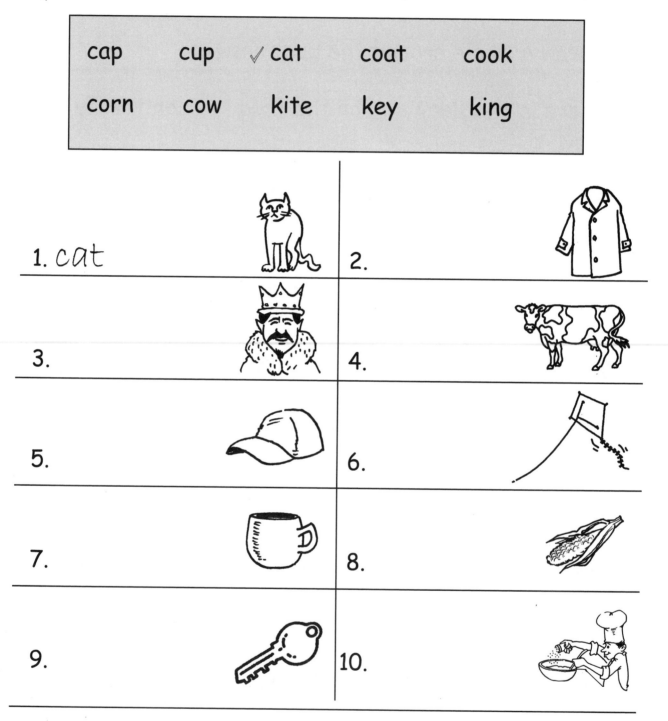

1. cat

2.

3.

4.

5.

6.

7.

8.

9.

10.

Mastery Test 2

Write the best word for each picture.

bag	bus	barn	brush	bird
box	book	bell	beard	bump

1.

2.

3.

4.

5.

6.

7.

8.

9.

10.

Mastery Test 3

✏ Write the best word for each picture.

man	men	map	mop	moon
moth	mouse	money	mouth	mother

1.

2.

3.

4.

5.

6.

7.

8.

9.

10.

Mastery Test 4

✏️ Write the best word for each picture.

sun	shell	shirt	store	sock
six	seven	sack	stairs	star

1.

2.

3.

4.

5.

6.

7.

8.

9.

10.

Mastery Test 5

✏️ Write the best word for each picture.

| puppy | pen | pin | pot | paddle |
| pillow | puddle | porch | purse | pig |

1. _____

2. _____

3. _____

4. _____

5. _____

6. _____

7. _____

8. _____

9. _____

10. _____

Mastery Test 6

Write the best word for each picture.

ant	animals	arm	arrow	ear
egg	octopus	orange	umbrella	umpire

1.

2.

3.

4.

5.

6.

7.

8.

9.

10.

Word List: New Words in Book Five

airplane	compass	fern	ink
Alabama	cook	fireman	
alarm	cotton	first	jaw
astronaut	crib	flap	joy
August	crooked	flapped	
automobile	curl	flea	
autumn		floss	kick
		for	kit
	dam	forest	knees
bad	daughter	fork	know
banjo	dead	forty	
barn	death	found	
beard	deck	froze	leather
bed	diamonds	full	leave
been	dig	fur	lie
beer	dirt		lies
bitten	disk		light
body	dock	germ	lips
bonnie	doctor	going	lived
boss	don't	gold	Louisiana
bottom	dot		love
bought			lump
bread		had	lung
bull	early	hall	
bump	ears	hawk	
butcher	egg	head	MacDonald
	eleven	healthy	may
	eyes	heavy	melon
call		her	met
catcher		herd	might
caught	fairy	honey	mile
chalk	fat	hood	mix
charming	faucet	hook	moo moo
clerk	fawn	hop	mop
collar	fence	horn	

© Elizabeth Claire, Inc. 2009 • ESL Phonics for All Ages: Book 5

next to	sad	umbrella
	saddle	umpire
	Saint Ives	
ocean	saucer	
octopus	sausage	verbs
of	sea	
once	see-saw	walk
one	seek	wall
orange	sell	wanted
	serve	was
	shark	wealthy
	shelf	weather
pack	shop	who
pair	sink	wife
pat	so	wig
paw	sorry	will
pearls	spear	willow
perch	spire	wings
picked	stile	wire
pig	store	wish
pocket		with
pull		wives
puppy		wood
purse	talk	written
	tan	
	tears	
quack	tell	
	thing	years
	third	young
rained	ticket	
ribs	times	
rob	together	
rubies	top	
	trips	
	true	
sack	turban	
sacks	turkey	

My Work

✓ Check your work.
✎ Write the number correct next to the page number.

Page	Correct / Total	Page	Correct / Total	Page	Correct / Total
5	_____ / 11	33	_____ / 8	75	_____ / 5
7	_____ / 13	34	_____ /18	76	_____ / 5
11	_____ / 8	36	_____ / 8	77	_____ / 7
12	_____ / 8	40	_____ / 7	82	_____ /13
13	_____ / 6	41	_____ / 8	83	_____ /12
19	_____ / 8	42	_____ /21	84	_____ /10
20	_____ / 8	43	_____ / 4	85	_____ /10
21	_____ / 6	46	_____ /17	86	_____ /10
23	_____ /5	49	_____ / 8	87	_____ /10
28	_____ / 8	55	_____ /18	88	_____ /10
29	_____ / 8	60	_____ / 8	89	_____ /10
30	_____ / 8	64	_____ / 8		
31	_____ / 7	69	_____ /10		
32	_____ /16	74	_____ / 7		

© Elizabeth Claire, Inc. 2009 · ESL Phonics for All Ages: Book 5